A Pastor's heart-wrenching true story of how his lovely wife, Karen, died twice and how God brought her back to him!

CODE BLUE X2

"As I rounded the corner, the blue light was on over the room I left my wife in!"

"Then it happened again…"

Pastor Gary L. & Lady Karen J. Pleasant

I

Code Blue X2

© 2013 – Pastor Gary L. Pleasant & Lady Karen J. Pleasant

ISBN-13: 978-1-61813-128-7

All Rights Reserved Under

International and Pan-American Copyright Conventions.

No part of this book may be used or reproduced in any manner

whatsoever without written permission except in the case of brief

quotations embodied in critical articles or reviews.

Printed in the United States by

Mira Digital Publishing

Chesterfield, Missouri 63005

I'm Alive! Thank God! I'm Alive!

Have you ever given much thought about if you were to die suddenly? Taken from your loved ones without a goodbye? Another laugh? Another joyful conversation? Well, if your answer is no, then you and I have something in common.

I would have never dreamed, and no one could have convinced me, that this would happen in my life. After all, I'm healthy! I wake up every day and go about my merry way! Then…what I thought was a routine visit to the emergency room on September 27, 2013, became a life-changing event for me.

On a daily basis, without fail, I thanked God for waking me up in the morning. However, October 2nd and 3rd has changed my perspective on how I thank God for the simple blessing of waking me up!! You see, on those dates I died… twice! But, Thank God! It was the miraculous life giving power of God that told death to, "Step back!", and He gave me another chance at life, twice! This experience has taught me how fragile life is.

On the weekend of November 2nd and 3rd, respectively, I took a lot of time to reflect on the miracles that God had given to us!

Life! Tears flowed down my face as I thought, "God didn't have to do it, but He did". I don't take it lightly for what He has done. He's given me another chance… He's given us another chance! To God be the Glory!

On Monday, November 4th as I awoke, I literally wanted to scream "I'm ALIVE!" The only reason I couldn't was because I didn't want to startle my husband as he rested peacefully by my side!!! Pastor Gary Pleasant, one of God's blessings.

Now each time I get up in the morning, every interaction with the love of my life, my husband, with my Mom, a sibling, friend, or member of our church, it brings a praise to my lips and reminds me again, by the grace of God… I'm alive!

Prayer: Lord, let the time that I have here on earth, reflect your love in everything I say and do. May the miracle that you have wrought in my life help someone gain a greater perspective on what it means to be ALIVE…Amen

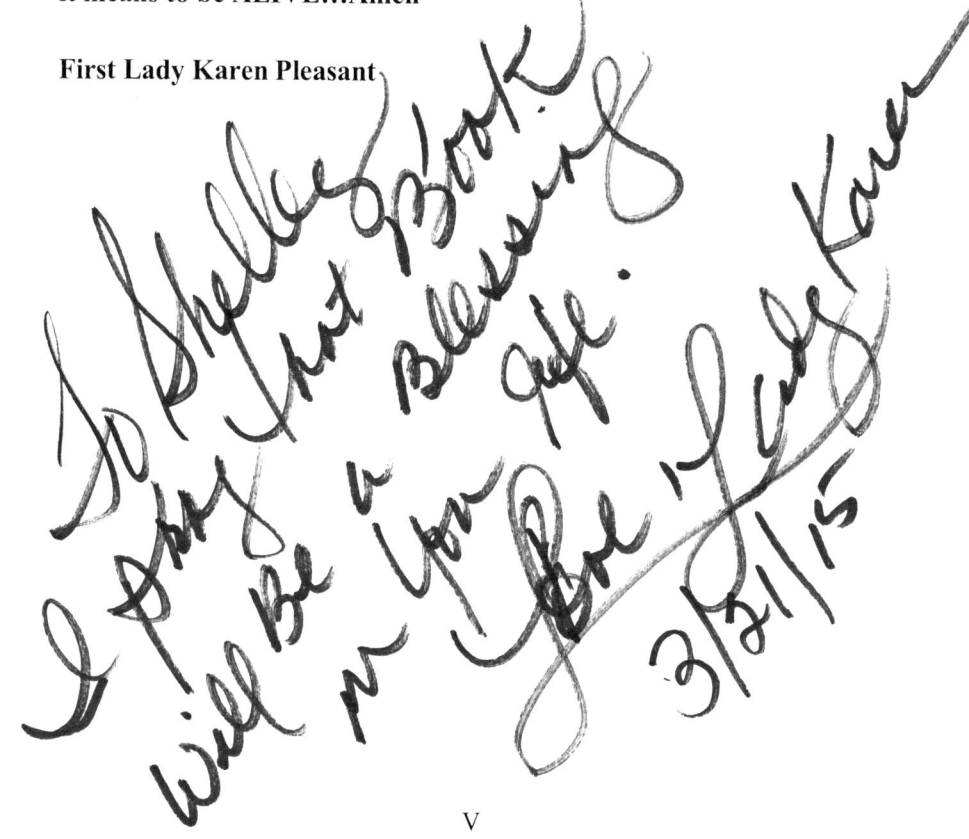

First Lady Karen Pleasant

Table of Contents

I'm Still Alive!..Lady Karen J. Pleasant
Foreword………………………………………..Author, Denise McCormick Baich
Introduction………………………………………….. Pastor Gary L. Pleasant

Chapters

Chapter 1 ……………………………………..................25th Anniversary
Chapter 2…………………………………………………..Meet the Pleasants
Chapter 3……………………………………… Just Routine, We Thought
Chapter 4……………………………………………………..In It Together
Chapter 5………………………..Just Wanted to See Her Smile Again
Chapter 6……………………………………….Things Start to Get Better
Chapter 7……………....Dedication……………………………...So Grateful
Chapter 8…………………………………………………………....Turbulence
Chapter 9……………………………………………………………...Truce!
Chapter 10……………………………………………………….Isaiah 43:5
Chapter 11………………....Defined…………….....................Code Blue
Chapter 12………………………………………….Room 662, That's My Room!
Chapter 13…………………………………..A Glad Dash to Trauma ICU
Chapter 14……………………………………………………Staff Elevator
Chapter 15…………………………………………………….Family Affair
Chapter 16……………………………………………………...By Her Side
Chapter 17……………………………………….....................Raspberry Shirt
Chapter 18……………………………………………………....ANGEL?
Chapter 19……………....Dedication………………."Poetry in Motion"
Chapter 20……………………………….....................I Didn't Get to Say Goodbye
Chapter 21……………………………………….....................Not Once, But Twice!
Chapter 22……………………………………………….The FACTS!
Chapter 23……………………………………………….Never the Same

Poem by Author, Denise McCormick Baich
Telling the Story through Pictures

FOREWORD

It was a beautiful fall Sunday morning in November and I was driving forty-five minutes to Florissant, Missouri to visit New Life Christian Church. Normally, I would be driving five minutes from my home to sing in the church choir, listen to the message within the sermon, home for a wonderful Sunday breakfast, and then get some laundry done. A fairly trivial day, right? Not today. Today *would not be trivial.* Today, as God often will have it, *OUR* plans are not *His* plans. I was happily delivering the first edit of Pastor Gary Pleasant's new book, "Code Blue!"

You should know that Pastor Gary Pleasant and First Lady Karen Pleasant are almost always wearing smiles. It is as if they know something wonderful about someone that they can't quite get a handle on yet. All of those who have the privilege to know the Pleasants experience this grin. It's a smile similar to the moments just before a birthday surprise, or just before a proposal when someone is down on one knee, or the expression when someone is announcing, "We are expecting!" to long-awaiting grandparents… It is a smile that just busts at the seams. For the Pleasants, it's the smile they wear just before they tell you about the many ways God loves us, how we are all His children. How, even in the darkest moments, God's light *will* find us… it's the beaming smile they wear just before they tell you, "We love you more."

They are amazing people with hearts that have been spiritually refined and shine as brilliant as gold. And their love for one another is something to truly treasure and strive for in our own relationships. They set an example unmatched in my experience.

God has provided the gift of poetry for me and through this and many gifts; I believe God has blessed both the Pleasants and me with a growing friendship.

How, you might ask? Less than a week prior to my beautiful Sunday drive to New Life Christian Church, Pastor Pleasant contacted me at

"Denise, I would really like to make an appointment for my wife and I to come in." In addition to poetry, I work at a spa. "Of course!" I replied and went to work getting them on the schedule.

Pastor Pleasant's voice settled into an audible gentleness I could actually feel over the phone. "Denise, I have to tell you… my wife coded on me twice…" As he told me the details my concentration waned and I had to ask him to repeat what he had just said. "I have written a book about this and God has impressed in my spirit to contact you for assisting us with editing this book." It had been a matter of just a few weeks since Pastor Pleasant had almost lost his precious Lady. I had to wrap my head around what could have possibly been. I had edited articles, but never a book. "Of course, I am honored to help," rolled off my tongue.

When they arrived a day later, my first desire was to wrap my arms around Lady Karen. To just take in her presence and selfishly let all my senses know she was still with us. She was visibly cautious and tired, but she still managed her fabulous smile. As I looked to Pastor Gary, he too looked concerned but truly blessed, and there was that smile.

As Karen settled into her appointment, Pastor Pleasant and I spoke more in depth about what had happened. He also spoke of how such an amazing experience had to be shared and he then discussed to what extent he would like my assistance in this project. I was so touched by the calling and his trust.

Pastor's accounting of those few days and hours when his wife, Karen, flat-lined will touch the heart and soul of anyone that reads this story. I believe it also stirs in someone the urgency to be prepared… be ready for their own "Code Blue". Whether it is a physical trial such as Lady Karen's or an emotional or spiritual "Code Blue", this… someday… will be you.

This is a story of profound faith and miracles. It is a moment in which we can all be assured… God is always there.

And my drive to Florissant? It was an awesome Sunday. And it was a special Sunday. My friend, Pastor Gary Pleasant walked hand in hand into the sanctuary with his wife, First Lady Karen Pleasant. It was and will *definitely* be worth the drive.

Introduction

As Pastor of a Church, I've visited many hospitals and have also had my share of personal stays in them. One thing I've noticed about hospitals is they are designed to make their visitors and patients feel warm and welcome. Beautiful landscaped waterfalls, spiritual writings on the walls, and lovely gift shops; all are breathtaking. Then there is the quiet aspect of a hospital; small Chapels for families that need to whisper a desperate prayer for their loved one. Small rooms that allow families tight intimate non-invaded spaces. Everyone within the hospital seems to be trained to respect each individual's "Moment" in these small spaces.

Rarely do you experience loud obnoxious behavior in a hospital. Occasionally you see loved ones carrying flowers with a concerned look on their face. Then there are moments that you see quiet grieving, only to assume that their loved one may not have made it, leaving you silently wondering what to do next. In these moments you want to offer a word of encouragement but the code of silence and respect for one's "Moment" keeps you from interrupting their solitude.

When experiencing these encounters, you walk down the corridors of the hospital or leave the elevator wondering what happened in that person's or family's life. Who did that family just lose or what life altering circumstance does that family have to cope with? All of this activity is occurring in a place that offers a sense of serenity; a place that you often see Chaplains passing by, no doubt, on their way to quietly pray or encourage another family.

During my wife's recent stay in a local hospital, we discovered something else about this code of silence and respect given to those in or visiting the hospital. Like other aspects of the hospital, what we discovered was this certain action is non-threatening to its guest; it is designed to prevent panic and intimidation.

Often, the average unsuspecting person visiting a hospital has no clue that a major crisis is taking place. An individual, with the most polite voice announces publicly over the intercom; "Code Blue 6th floor room 662." Announces again, "Code Blue 6th floor room 662." Reading these words does no justice over hearing them. No other information is announced. Precision and quickness is then on a mission to save a life! To the untrained ear this announcement means nothing. To those that are trained to respond and react to it, it can disrupt a calm world and transform into a life and death situation. They move with urgency and accuracy. They move to resolve the disruption of this otherwise quiet world… the hospital.

My reference to a quiet world is not meant to demean in any way the great work that doctors and staff do on an ongoing basis. I totally understand the day to day challenges they face helping their patients. My intentions are to inform those that read this book of the heightened state of the hospital staff that is trained to respond to a "Code Blue". Since the time my wife coded, we now have a new perspective on the meaning.

Here is our Story…

Chapter 1
25th Anniversary

By the time a couple reaches 25 years of marriage they are usually spending their celebration of love on a beach or in some romantic location. Ironically, we celebrated our 25th anniversary in a local hospital. I was hospitalized for 13 days in May, 2013 with a possible fatal condition. God miraculously healed me when actually the doctor's professional opinion was that I should definitely have surgery. I will discuss that in my next book because *this* book is about the experience my wife and I had during her 13 day stay in a hospital right down the street from where I was admitted. During my stay in the hospital, the staff went out of their way to make our 25th Silver Anniversary "Golden." The staff came and decorated our room while my wife was away. The celebration was so memorable because I was with my wife, Karen. They even published our story in the BJC Hospital News Letter, with a distribution of 29,000 readers, (see BJC June edition letter, 2013), our story was shared with many.

Karen and I have this bond that if either one of us are in the hospital, we request an additional bed for the other to sleep in. Yes, 25 years later, we are still in love. Let me go back just a bit to help you understand how this all got started.

I had given my life to the Lord at the age of 21. About a year into my walk with God, I was attending a Church service that was also attended by Karen. When I walked into the Church Karen was up singing, *"Never Say No to Jesus"*. It was then that the Lord Jesus spoke to my heart and informed me that this young lady was to be my wife. I couldn't say no to Jesus. ☺ Well, truthfully, I was not interested nor prepared for being married at that time but God was revealing to me His plans for my life.

After two years of intense study of the Word of God, my human desire for companionship kicked in. My heart went toward the beautiful young lady the Lord had revealed to me two years prior. She was love struck the moment she saw me. ☺ After dating for a short period, I asked her Father for her hand in marriage and he consented.

Chapter 2
Who are we? Meet the Pleasants

As I pen this book, we have been married for 25 years since that wonderful day, May 28, 1988. I've decided to ask a few of our friends and loved ones to paint a picture for you so that you may know us a little better. As you read the following, please understand that I did not influence the expressions or comments of our friends or loved ones. Their statements are of their volition.

Pastor David L. Baker (Best Friend)

It is with honor and great pleasure that I take the time to share a few thoughts about my closest friends, Pastor Gary & 1st Lady Karen Pleasant. I've had the privilege of knowing the two of them before they were joined in marriage and even knew them individually before they knew one another. What stands out in my mind about the two of them is that even when they were in their pre-teen years, they both displayed Great Passion. Pastor Pleasant was so passionate about playing football more than anyone I've ever seen at his age; such determination, commitment, confidence, belief and will to win. Lady Pleasant exhibited the same passion but hers was in her singing for the Lord. I would always enjoy her singing in the choir at her Dad's Church; giving it all she had; as we would say in our day, "bringing down the house". I've never labeled myself as matchmaker but would like to think that I had a role in what I consider would become the greatest union and marriage that I've ever witnessed (and I've seen a lot of them).

From this God ordained marriage I have witnessed some Mighty, Marvelous & Miraculous things; as Church Planter & Pioneers, Entrepreneurs , Counselors, Men & Women Outreach Ministries, Author, Pastor Fellowships, Youth Outreach, Children Ministries just to name a few and the accolades will continue from their union. In my eyes, I deem them as the greatest model and example of a Christian Marriage in my era. On a very personal note, out of all the hats these two wear, the greatest one for me is when they say Pastor Baker is our Friend. I am so grateful for their friendship, because if it weren't for their friendship during the darkest day of my life (passing of my wife) I don't believe that I would be alive today. So as you read this book, I assure you that there will be no doubt that you will discover that Gary loves Karen, and Karen loves Gary. Together they are our modern day, Romeo & Juliet.

Love you both,
PASTOR D.L.BAKER (FFL)

Curt Cavendar (Very Dear Friend/Brother)

You never know what the day holds or who you will encounter as the time passes. I once thought luck had a lot to do with my life, but would later be proven wrong by two of GOD's special people. I've never been a people- person or even an easy person to get to know, but when I met the Pleasants, I felt at peace. I've known them for a couple of years now and that feeling has only grown stronger. I no longer have two acquaintances. I no longer just have two friends. I now have two family members.

I've met thousands of people over the years in the restaurant business, but Pastor P and Lady P were different from the rest. I would stop working just to have an opportunity to sit and talk. It didn't matter what mood I was in, I always felt better after speaking with them. We've had some pretty in depth conversations over the years about my religious beliefs, or lack thereof, as well as life in general. They told me about their faith and always said they were praying for me. For someone that had their doubts about the subject, I didn't really know how to respond.

As time passed, I made a comment to Pastor. "Who would have ever thought that our paths would cross?" He looked at me and said "I know who, GOD." That very simple response really made me think. It was like a light bulb went off and I could respond; you're right! It wasn't luck that these two people walked into my life. It wasn't luck that when I needed it most I received a phone call or text. It was GOD.

So no, I would not have planned for our paths to cross because we're so different, but luckily GOD is in control and He knew that I needed them in my life. I thank GOD for giving me the opportunity to get to know the Pleasants. They are two of the most precious and genuine people I've ever met.

Thanks,
Curt Cavender

LaShawn Richardson *"D"* (Niece/Spiritual Daughter)

"The Pleasants"

There is so much that I could say about these two people, as individuals and as a couple, but, for the sake of time I will try to be brief. I've known both Pastor and Lady Pleasant as family since before I can remember. Lady Pleasant is my father's sister and Pastor Pleasant is Lady Pleasant's husband. I guess, technically this would make Lady Pleasant my aunt and Pastor Pleasant my uncle. However, even before we were as close as we are now, I never saw either of them this way...

Lady Pleasant played a pivotal role in my upbringing from birth. My parents divorced early in my life and I have no memories of them together as husband and wife. Nonetheless, I have very fond memories of a strong support system, which would have been missing a vital part without the love and support shown to me by Lady Pleasant.

She was my very first fashion icon! She never lagged behind in the style department, still doesn't to this day. She took out time with me from infancy to teach me important lessons about being lady-like, being serious about my education, and most of all about how to live in a way that is pleasing to God. I guess something's never change. I can honestly look back over my life and say that she has been there every step of the way and I am so grateful. Without her contribution to my life I am certain that I would not be the woman that I am today.

Pastor Pleasant, although not related by blood, is no less family to me than my own parents. He is also part of the fond memories of my childhood. My cousins and I often share how his conversation was always so meaningful, even when we were children! He seemed to never miss an opportunity to give a nugget of wisdom, (which must have come from his heart because it reached mine). No matter what season of life I was in, he always reminded me of my worth and how I deserved the best that God had to offer in my life. Now, more than ever he is a rock of support for me. He is never too busy to talk, listen, or deal with whatever it is that's going on in my life. This means so much coming from a man who would need a state-of-the-art, new and improved, custom-made hat rack to hold all the numerous hats that he wears. He is an irreplaceable force in my life and for him, I am grateful.

As a couple, they are a force to be reckoned with. They are a model couple for me and so many others. Yet, they are so humble about how God has blessed them in marriage. The love that they show each other is a true example of the love of Christ. In my community, there weren't many couples that could be looked up to in the way that they are. I have had the privilege of a close enough relationship with the both of them that I would have noticed if the mutual love and respect that they display is an act. That is why I am a witness that what they share is the real thing! The couple that you meet in public is the exact same couple in their private life.

I have never seen such cohesiveness in a marriage. Having the Pleasants in my life has given me an example of just how beautiful marriage can be when you trust God.

I love you both from the deepest depths of my heart and I thank you for being my spiritual parents.

Love Always,
LaShawn Richardson *"D"*

Our hope is the statements provided help you gain a better picture of who we are. We believe our story will resonate a little deeper in your heart if we were made more personal.

Chapter 3
Just Routine, We Thought

Over the years of our marriage, Karen and I have had to go to the emergency room on different occasions for one thing or another. I have had to go more often than my wife. So when my wife became ill the last week of September, we both were conditioned to making just routine emergency room visits. You know what I'm talking about. The usual doctor checking you out, running a few tests, sending you home with a 30 day prescription… just routine. To our surprise September 27, 2013, was not going to be a routine visit. Let me first explain my wife's attitude toward hospitals and medication. SHE DOESN'T LIKE THEM! Not one bit! I actually need the patience of Job just to convince her to take an Advil. For Karen to take vitamins is like running a marathon. I should invent a game called, "How long can you wait?" Through this game we would all be taught that when you love someone you just smile, shake your head, and stick to it and we could all be winners!

As I stated earlier, my wife had taken ill near the end of September during a trip to Columbus, Ohio. We were not sure how long Karen had been sick because there were never any symptoms. But we do know that while she was in Ohio to support our nephew (due to the loss of his beautiful Fiancée a little over a month before their wedding day) is when my wife began to experience symptoms. Even while her own body was in pain she unselfishly supported our nephew and his Fiancée's family. Karen even allowed our niece, who travelled with her, to do some shopping. Karen never let our niece know what was going on in her own body. My wife is just that kind of person.

When Karen returned home on Tuesday I noticed that she was very lethargic. As First Lady of New Life Christian Church, she is very active in our ministry. But on this day I suggested she stay home and rest from our Tuesday night Prayer service.

Again, on Wednesday, she was still very tired. I thought it may be because our schedule had been pretty hectic but I became concerned enough to make an appointment with our doctor. The appointment was for that following Friday morning, however she began to experience chills on Thursday. She had now been sick in the bed for the last three days and we were hoping that rest would help her through this ordeal.

Friday morning we awoke early to prepare for her scheduled doctor's appointment. Karen drank a glass of orange juice hoping it would help her get through the morning and calm her stomach. The reaction to the OJ was… not good. Everything in her stomach began to come up! This left her very weak, so I called our doctor's office and informed them of what was taking place. They told me to get her to the emergency room *right away*! It weighed heavy on my heart to see my wife so weak.

Like so many other times before in our lives, Karen and I worked together and managed to get her to the emergency room.

After being examined in the emergency room, Karen was admitted immediately. Ironically, we had just experienced this in May when I had to be admitted to the hospital.

We truly live by our marriage vows, "In sickness and in health". On that occasion it was our 25th year of marriage. At this point in our lives we should be living it up! Sailing off into Bliss-land and not spending more time in the hospital! What we thought was just going to be a routine visit was now turning out to be the most challenging time of our lives together.

Chapter 4
In it Together

During my stay in the hospital I had requested a bed for my wife so she could be right by my side. This is a true reflection of how our marriage has been from day one. We always do things together. And when I say always, I mean *always!*

The first few nights in the hospital we were in the Critical Care Unit (CCU) where there was a couch/ sleeper and a recliner available. Then a few days later we were moved to the sixth floor of the hospital. While in the CCU, Karen experienced severe pain. Oh, my goodness! How I so wished with all my heart that it was me instead of her. At night I would rub her stomach to help soothe her until she could finally fall asleep. And as she slept, I would pray over her. All I wanted was for her to get better.

I remember so vividly going home after a couple of days to shower and change my clothes. While at home, I experienced the sick empty feeling of my wife not being there. I remember a song Luther Vandross sang years ago entitled *"A House is not a Home"*. The structure where I stood at that moment was previously known as "Our home", but on this day I did not feel right in this place. It was not "home", because my Karen was not with me. It had to be the emptiest feeling I had ever experienced in my life. The best way to explain it is, "EERIE SILENCE!" No air was moving, no sounds of water, just plain cold silence. Something just wasn't right! I had the terrible feeling that my wife could possibly not come home with me again. I wanted out of that house because Karen wasn't there. I wasn't panicky; I just wanted to be back by her side. You see, together, we make our home. Our home is warm with one another. It is full when we are in it together! So as I sat at the end of our bed, my heart was empty. For some reason in my mind, for one horrible moment, I began to ponder what my life would be like without her.

Until this point, Karen had only been hospitalized with acute pancreatitis. Little did I know that I was, for the moment, living with thoughts that I would soon experience! I did not like it! Not one bit! And yet... the thoughts were *so real*. A few years earlier I walked very closely with a dear friend that lost his wife. This experience allowed me to literally feel what could have been my friend's reality. With all due respect to my friend, I left that house knowing a little better what my friend must have gone through. I snapped out of that, I had to. I needed to pack some of Karen's things (and I needed to concentrate because I wanted to do this task like she would have for me), and then get back to the hospital to be with Karen.

Chapter 5
Just Wanted to See Her Smile Again

When I arrived back at the hospital, Karen was still experiencing tremendous discomfort and pain. I wanted to take her mind off how she was feeling so as I unpacked some of the things we needed, I explained in detail how I had tried to pack for her like she had always packed for us. I told her how I had remembered small things. Truth be told, when I was home I noticed the luggage that she had taken to Ohio was still resting on the floor. I took some of her little make up bags along with night clothes and neatly placed them into one of our mid-sized shoulder bags. (Even when she wasn't there, she still had a hand in the packing).

It was a proud moment for me as I shared with Karen the attention to detail I had put into the things I had thought to bring for her. Well... I was on a roll until she asked for her night scarf that she liked to wear to bed. Ahhh! Man!!!! (That's exactly how I felt...) But she quickly reassured me by saying, "That's alright, Honey. You tried," with a gentle nod and an appreciative smile. My wife, always fixing things. But now my mission had become finding her a night scarf. Right away, I took the elevator to the lobby, dashed into the gift shop and purchased my wife a pink scarf, her favorite color. I just wanted to make Karen happy and see her smile again.

Chapter 6
Things Start to Get Better

After spending a few days in the CCU, my wife's vitals started to look better. They were managing her pain with meds and she was becoming more stable. As she started feeling better Karen was transferred to the sixth floor, room number 662. What I am about to say is not to slight or discredit any of the staff, but I noticed the nurse to patient ratio is higher on the regular floors than in the Critical Care Units. I'm not sure if this is standard procedure for all hospitals. I believe it was one nurse and tech to every six patients as opposed to one to three in the CCU. On the sixth floor we encountered wonderful nurses and techs. Our minds were then focused on the next step, which was going home.

Now, we weren't too anxious to get home without my wife being totally well, but it seemed like that was the next logical step for us. We requested an additional bed so that I could stay in room 662 with her. This room was equipped with a hospital bed for Karen and one recliner, for me. Our niece, who is like a daughter to us, (we are like her second parents), was in on the request as well. She had witnessed how her Momma C-ta (Karen) was accommodated when I was in the hospital. So she kindly asked if they could then provide a bed for me. Well, she was informed that we could have a bed, so we waited… My wife managed to finally find sleep, so at about 4AM the chair and I had had enough of each other. I went home to try and muster a couple of hours of sleep. Yes, I went to the "Empty, Silent, Eerie House!"

Karen was extremely disappointed that I had not received a bed, so while I was gone she asked one of the wonderful techs to please have a bed delivered for her husband. To appreciate why this is so important, you should know just a little bit more about me. The size ratio between me and the hospital recliner was vast. As a young man, I played football and the average reclining chair will not accommodate my stature very well for long periods of time.

When I returned to the hospital, the room had received a makeover. A very nice bed was waiting for me when I entered the room. This meant I would not have to leave her again until we would be going home together. This is another reason why I appreciate Karen so very much. Even while sick, she still was looking after me.

Chapter 7
So Grateful

I would like to take a moment to express how grateful we are to our New Life Christian Church Family. As my wife and I experienced this ordeal, they prayerfully enabled me to take care of her. My Church Family understands that my First Ministry is to my wife. So as we traveled through this journey, they prayerfully waited and are still waiting for the Lord to finish His plan for us and our Ministry. I am so humbled and honored to Pastor such a wonderful group of people. The young Ministers and the Women of our ministry are awesome! You never know what you have on your side until you go into battle. What we've discovered is the people in our ministry are solid and mature in their faith. You see, as we go through, they are going through also. Thank You, New Life Family! We will always love you MORE!!!

Chapter 8
Turbulence!

I remember flying on a plane and everything seemed to be going pretty smooth. Then all of the sudden, the plane would shake violently and things would get bumpy. This is called Turbulence! This attention-getting action is caused by a storm and/or wind in the upper atmosphere. Truth be told, nobody I know likes turbulence. But this is what I began to feel after things started to turn for my wife. An ensuing battle to regulate her blood sugar was about to take a nasty turn.

First off, because of the battle with her pancreas, Karen was forced to eat only ice chips to allow her pancreas to rest. I found this experience so interesting because this is exactly what I had gone through just four months prior. Karen had commented to others that she was so glad that I was a man that had spent so much time fasting. Fasting had conditioned me to handle my situation with ease. She had also fasted before but not the thirty and forty days that I had spent fasting. So as I watched her battle the pains in her body, with only ice chips to eat coupled with blood sugar battles, I wanted so badly to take her place in that bed.

There has been a lot of damage done to the male image. Satan is mad because Man is made in God's Image, but I consider myself a real man and I wanted to do what any real man would do. Take the Turbulence from my wife and put it on myself. Karen's brother, Elder Cedric Richardson, said the exact same thing when he came to visit. "I just wished I could have taken my sister's place." My brother-in-law for these 25 plus years has always been pretty mellow, but for the first time in my life I witnessed him with tears in his eyes declaring that he wanted to take his sister's pain. Even as I pen this statement my eyes are flooding with tears because her brother's love touched me so deeply.

At this point, my wife had been stuck with needles countless times. Troubles with finding veins for IV's began to surface. Remember, we are dealing with an individual that hates taking a simple Advil.

It is so painful when you feel helpless. When you want to take the pain away and you can't... THAT CAN PHYSICALLY HURT! I thought when we brought her to the hospital on the 27th of September that she would be there for a minute and then back home again. We had not prepared for *this*. What we were dealing with was becoming too big for us!

Have you ever prayed and things became worse? Things were getting worse! Efforts to get my wife's blood regulated seemed futile. Her pain began to increase and she was literally "running on empty." No food, just ice chips. I would pray as I fed her ice chips, just to try to encourage her. I longed for her to find some comfort. I needed her to have some normalcy. I needed GOD to hear my prayers!

I must admit, you can appear calm on the outside, but inwardly you are literally *SCREAMING*, "God, PLEASE HELP!!!"

Chapter 9
TRUCE!

The word "Truce" is an interesting word. It means an agreement between enemies or opponents to stop fighting or arguing for a certain time. Its synonyms are; ceasefire, suspension of hostilities, peace and let up. Her blood sugar seemed to do just that! It ceased being high. It suspended its hostilities. It stopped fighting and "let up." They managed to get her blood sugar down to a reasonable number. Now, the efforts turned to *maintaining* that number. Better yet, keep her blood stable.

I remember on the morning of October 2, 2013, we were celebrating this great TRUCE with her blood sugar. Our conversation turned serious when we began to discuss the risk of my wife's blood sugar bottoming out. I had shared with my wife that I was familiar with this happening to people I knew and how they would eat a candy bar or drink an Orange Crush soda. I shared this because I knew the danger of low blood sugar and the importance of getting it to rise quickly so that a person would be stable. I clearly remember the DANGER expressed by the nurse that was on duty that evening.

Chapter 10
Isaiah 43:5

At about 7PM in the evening I decided to go downstairs to get myself something to eat. I also felt the need to take a moment to rest my mind. I was truly making an effort to keep myself strong for my wife. I love having moments of solitude; a time when I can listen to the voice of God. Over the years I've learned to cherish these moments wherever I am. So, I went down to the cafeteria leaving Karen up in room 662.

I must admit, the challenges they had getting my wife's blood sugar down had me confident that she would not be a candidate to bottoming out. I was so glad that her numbers were close to normal. I finished up my chicken salad sandwich and as I started walking back to the elevators, I detoured to the lobby that offered so much serenity. I took a seat right by the gift shop that was now closed. It was empty and very quiet. At about 8:15 I decided to go across the lobby and sit in a more secluded area because the breeze from the door made me uncomfortable.

As I took my seat I looked up on the wall and saw Isaiah 43:5a, **"Do not be afraid, for I am with you"**. This scripture for some reason had me in a trance-like state as I read it. It was as though my Spirit was eating supper for the night, literally dining on the contents! *I WAS MESMERIZED BY IT!* I recall saying aloud, "WOW!" After reading it, I called our praise and worship leader to see how rehearsal had gone and I was told it was POWERFUL! Powerful. I also spoke with my niece who shared the same thing. After speaking with the two of them, I thought it was time to make my way back up to the room. Knowing that the evening rehearsal had gone so well, knowing that Karen's battle with her blood sugar was at a truce, I was feeling a wonderful sense of calm as I made my way to room 662...

Chapter 11
Code Blue

I have discovered that hospitals have different codes they use. Some have codes for bad weather; codes for specific doctors and nurses; and codes for different emergency situations. This book is about a code used in this hospital. ***Code Blue:*** When this code is sounded, it is alerting a professionally trained staff that an individual is in need of resuscitation or has flat-lined (which could mean no heart beat or pulse). This call is a life or death call. As I stated in my introduction, this hospital makes these announcements in such a non-threatening manner. However, what goes on during a Code Blue is anything but non-threatening. Someone's life is on the line. Some patients have minutes; others have just seconds before being declared deceased. I must say it is a class act watching how this situation is handled by the hospital staff. I will detail later what goes on and how this looks in action. I have witnessed this twice. Poetry in motion...

Chapter 12
Room 662, that's My Room!

In my lifetime, I've had my name put into drawings hoping to hear it called. We have all gone to special dinners and during the night numbers are called for prize giveaways. Unfortunately, I've never heard my name or number called for any large prizes.

When I stepped off the elevator I made my way to our room. As I was entering, my cell phone rang. It was my sister, First Lady Angela Patton. I looked in on my wife and noticed she was facing the window. It appeared as though she was asleep; I will be sharing what was actually occurring with her later. So I eased out of the room hoping not to disturb her and spoke with my sister. I went back around the corner and took a seat in the lobby area located on the same floor. It was about 9PM. As I spoke with my sister I noticed three to four doctors and nurses running full speed down the hall. Apparently, a Code Blue had been announced along with the room number and floor, but due to my conversation with my sister, I did not hear this announcement. I shared with my sister, "I think someone has coded". My sister (who is a nurse) replied, "Yes, when someone codes, they announce "CODE BLUE". When my sister finished her explanation, I noticed two or three more doctors and nurses, running at full speed, passing right by me. The furthest thing from my mind was they were heading to room 662... our room...

"Let me go around the corner and see what's going on." WHEN I TURNED THE CORNER, THE BLUE LIGHT WAS ON OVER THE ROOM I LEFT MY WIFE IN...ROOM 662! I have to take a moment now, it is still so FRESH! I noticed that all the staff was rushing into our room. It was at least fifteen to twenty feet from the corner to room 662. To this day I cannot honestly tell you how I got there so fast. As I entered the room... I saw my WIFE! One of the nurses said respectfully, "Sir, you cannot come in here." I replied, "THAT'S MY WIFE!"

Remember? Isaiah 43:5a, "Don't be afraid, I am with you". I don't want to appear to be some spiritual giant, nor do I want you to think I'm super human. But... the PEACE of God was all over me and in me. I needed it for what I was about to hear and witness. As I stood about six feet from my wife the next words I heard resonated in my spirit deeper than any words I had ever heard before! "NO HEART BEAT, NO PULSE". Immediately my logic, common sense and every ounce of my intelligence SHOUTED WITHIN ME! "KAREN IS DEAD!" And I heard my mind shout back... "NO! NOT MY WIFE!"

So I noticed in that moment of time that it seemed like a thousand thoughts were in my head and each one required my undivided attention. I would like to walk you through a few of them.

1) I heard myself saying, "Not my wife, I can't live without her".
2) Thoughts of what would I do without her flooded my mind.
3) I noticed a man conducting CPR on Karen.
4) I heard the time keeper at the foot of Karen's bed counting...counting "How much time?" (This refers to minutes and seconds that my wife did not have her precious heartbeat).
5) I identified the individual with what looked like a small cell phone responding, "ONE MINUTE!"
6) I recognized the nurse that was on duty that evening standing in the corner with a glazed-over expression on her face.
7) I also recall looking directly into the eyes of the charge nurse that we had come to know during our stay.
8) I recall looking down at my phone and noticed that I hadn't hung up with my sister. I then brought the phone to my ear and said to my sister, "Its Karen", "I need you here!"
9) I dialed my best friend Pastor David Baker. His phone went directly to voice mail. I hung up the phone and heard them call out "TWO MINUTES!
10) Pastor Baker called me back, and as I answered the phone with the peace of God over me, he later told me I calmly said, "Baker, I need to get back with you". I thought I had told him I needed him there also, but maybe he had already hung up by then.

11) I heard them call out, "THREE MINUTES!"

12) I THEN WHISPERED TO GOD, "Lord, send my wife back". I didn't rebuke or bind the enemy. I did not speak in an unknown language; I just asked my Daddy in heaven to send my wife back. I couldn't live without her.

13) I then heard the Code Blue responders say, "Step back! All clear!" They then counted, "ONE, TWO, THREE…!" This is when they used a piece of equipment called a defibrillator. *This device is used during life threatening cardiac dysrhythmias, ventricular fibrillation and pulseless ventricular tachycardia. Defibrillation consists of delivering a therapeutic dose of electrical to the heart. This action depolarizes a critical mass of the heart muscle, terminates the dysrhythmia and allows normal sinus rhythm to be reestablished by the body's natural pacemaker, in the Sino atrial node of the heart.*

14) I noticed my wife's body jarring as each strong life-saving electrical current was sent through her delicate frame.

15) I recall them saying, "WE HAVE A PULSE!" THANK GOD! He heard my prayer! I will later share what the lead doctor said to me concerning prayer.

The moment they said, "WE HAVE A PULSE!" I called to my wife, "I'M HERE BABY, I'M HERE!" The female doctor that was standing by her bed turned to me, grabbed my hand, and said, "Talk to her". THIS WAS THE BEST CONVERSATION THAT I DON'T REMEMBER. I looked into her eyes and felt the terror that she was dealing with. As her eyes connected with mine she began to calm down. I remember sharing with Karen what was happening to her. With great fear, she was asking me questions. *"**What happened?**"* (Wide-eyed and breathless!) My wife does not like anything over her face or mouth, and the oxygen mask in addition to all the people surrounding her bed did not settle well with her. So, I prayerfully and gently assured her that everything was alright. She trusted me and what I was saying to her.

Chapter 13
A Glad dash to Trauma ICU

I know most of us have heard the quote, "A Mad Dash". Well, no one was mad here. I was only glad. Glad that I would be getting another chance to speak to Karen. As we are moving out of room 662 and headed to the Trauma ICU, I heard some team members saying, "He can't go!" But, for some reason, they did not attempt to move me away from my wife. So, like a scene from the *television show ER*, we were moving down the corridors of the hospital. Karen suddenly let out a loud scream. I heard the doctor that had previously taken me by the hand say, "THAT'S GOOD!" (Medically). What my wife did next literally blew my mind... She began to PRAISE GOD! I heard her say, "THANK YOU, JESUS!" Then she said, "HALLELUJAH!" I then heard my mind say, "THAT'S GOOD!" (Spiritually)

Let me explain why the doctor said it was good for my wife to scream out. Considering the entire trauma she went through and all the CPR that was applied to her upper torso, the scream was an indicator that she was alert and, just maybe, no ribs were broken during CPR and most of all, her lungs were not crushed or punctured. I was told later by one of the nurses that normally when a person suffers ventricular defibrillation they are on a breathing tube for at least three days. The same nurse told me that in all her years of nursing, she has never seen anyone come out of this type of cardiac arrest, alert and talking like my Karen. In her words, "She is a **MIRACLE**".

Chapter 14
Staff Elevator

We were now approaching the staff elevators. These elevators are only to be used by hospital staff. I truly understand the importance of this rule after our ordeal. Again, I heard someone say, "He can't get on!" Once again, no one made any effort to tell me, "Sir, can you back away please?" I want to assure you that I was not being rude or obnoxious with the hospital staff. I was focused only on what was going on with Karen.

As the elevator doors opened, I was leaning over my wife and she began telling me that she loved me and I was telling her the same. Her next move shocked me. She began kissing me as the elevator doors were closing. My mind was saying, "Girl, what are you doing? We are not supposed to be doing this!" But in truth it was a joy to kiss her again. All of this was occurring at the same time I was squeezing into the staff elevator. She didn't believe this portion of the story until we went back to the Trauma Unit and one of the nurses on duty the first night she coded said, "Girl, you gave us a scare!", then she told Karen," I remember you kissing on your husband on the way to the Trauma Unit."
☺

While closed in the elevator, we were still sharing how much we love one another. The elevator doors then opened and we had to stop kissing as the crowd moved toward the Trauma Unit, located on the fourth floor. As we were approaching the unit, (My Church members tell me I see everything), I noticed her foot was hanging off the bed while we were heading toward a counter in the Trauma Unit hallway. I alerted one of the nurses at the end of her bed to, "WATCH HER FOOT!" The nurse looked up at me as she placed Karen's foot back up on the bed. Her expression was one of, "Who is this guy and how is it that he is so calm and alert?"

Later that morning one of the nurses speaking with us said,"Your husband is a good husband because other husbands would not have done what he did. My wife asked, "What do other husbands do?" The nurse said, "They would go into the other room and just wait." Then she said, "When you all came through the doors of the Trauma Unit, we actually thought your husband was a Doctor giving out orders, until someone said that's her husband." My wife and I just smiled.

Chapter 15
Family Affair

Let's return to the night of the first CODE BLUE... As the staff stabilized my wife, I called my wife's Mother to inform her of what had taken place and also to let her know that I had already contacted our head Deacon and his wife and they were on their way to pick her up.

I noticed my Sister Angela had arrived as I was calling each one of my wife's siblings. One by one I was calling them. Beginning with the oldest first; I called her oldest Sister, First Lady Kathy Franklin. I then called her oldest brother, Elder Clyde Richardson, who literally travels around the country as a Specialist for a major corporation. I believe he was in Baltimore heading to New York. Her family members dropped everything, and one by one made their way to the bedside of their dear Sister.

After having five brothers born before Karen, she was the family's "Cookie". They all love one another, but it was just special when Karen was born. So upon each one of her siblings' arrival, the moments were touching. Please know this serves no disrespect to any of my in-laws, but I will never forget the look on my wife's face when her eldest brother walked into her room the next night. So tender, so heartwarming, the smile behind the tears in each of their faces will forever be etched in my mind. As he approached Karen's bed, tears running down his cheeks and her's as well, he bent down and kissed her, and then immediately began to pray. Laying his hands on her head, both of them looked to the Master for a touch that only can be given by God Himself.

Each moment with her siblings was touching but it was something about her eldest brother coming from so far away, in the middle of the night. Karen's eldest Sister and I were both in tears that moment. Lady Kay, thank you for another one of my wife's most memorable moments. In her words, "When Kathy washed my face and hands I will never forget how gentle and loving she was.

As she, with the utmost tenderness, slowly washed my face and each finger one at a time. I will never forget that in the midst of my agony, I was comforted by my Big Sister." And to each one of her siblings; First Lady Kathy Franklin and Pastor Donald Franklin, Elder Cedric and Dr Carrie Richardson, Elder Lamont, Pastor Quinton, Elder Randle, Eddie Lee Jr and First Lady Ramona Miles. To Mother Junetta Richardson, who, on the first night her daughter coded, called and prayed with Karen moments before. Thanks for interceding in prayer for Karen. Thanks, Mom! The love this family displayed needs to be shared with the whole world. I am so blessed to have each of you in my life. This also includes Lashawn Richardson who is always by her Momma C-ta's side, as well as our strong Nephew, RJ Richardson, who, although suffering the loss of his fiancé a month prior, was by his aunt's side. To all the dear relatives that drove up from Arkansas or phoned; thank you ever so much!

To the members of my immediate family; thank you for being there to comfort us. Angela Patton, who has always been a leader for our family since losing our Mother, was there doing her motherly thing for me. In my wife's words, "Angela, I thank you for being so gracious on the night of my first Code Blue". My oldest brother, whom my wife just loves, closed his shop to be by our side. The one that causes my wife to weep each time he is in her presence…you both know what that's about. Thanks for sitting with her, allowing me to leave to take care of church and home business. I am so proud to have you as my big brother. I'll never forget you saying to me, "Whatever you need, I am here for you". Love you, Brother. To my Sister-in-Law Debra, you have the true heart of a servant. Dawn, John, Stephanie and Sean; thanks for being there when we needed it the most. The love that surfaced during this event can never be packed away or buried again. Family took on a whole new meaning for us during this ordeal.

Chapter 16
By Her Side

As the Trauma team did their thing, I did mine. I stayed by Karen's side the whole night. I watched over her every hour, minute, and second. I prayed. We shared. I sang. We touched hands ever so gently. Those well-meaning individuals that thought I should get rest myself did not understand that being by her side was the best rest I could ask for. The events that occured earlier kept replaying in my mind. I was not in the room when it all started, and I was not going to be out of the room if it happened again! Stay tuned...

As I mentioned before, I would share with you what was going on with Karen as I was entering into the room at 9pm. Well, she was facing the window and appeared to be resting. This was far from what actually was going on. My wife was in the process of coding at that very moment. She shared with me later that she felt so weak. The very moment I was entering into the room when my sister called, I remember the tech being in there. He was there to check her blood level. It was at this time that Karen began to inform the tech that she, "JUST NEEDED HER HUSBAND". Can you imagine if God would have taken her and I was left with her request? *"I JUST NEED MY HUSBAND."* I have put that in my "what-if" bucket. One day I plan to write about the "what-if's" of our story, currently it is still very troubling for me to process that... Thank you, God, for sending her back!

Again, my phone rang and I had backed out of the door so that I would not disturb my wife. As it happened, she was actually looking for me. She informed the tech that she needed her husband and he informed her that I was out in the hallway on the phone. As everyone knows, I would have dropped *any call* at my wife's request. No one is more important than my wife.

But the fact is the tech knew her blood had bottomed out and he was not going to leave her alone in that room. Karen remembers him calling the

Nurse to inform her of how low her blood sugar had dropped. The nurse requested the tech check Karen's blood sugar again. He does and discovers that the reading was accurate. By this time my wife was passing out, no longer able to ask for me. Before losing consciousness her mind went to the sweet Orange Crush soda I had talked about earlier that day. She remembers the joy she had thinking that she was going to be sipping on the Orange Crush soda.

To fill in the rest of the story I took a moment days later to go back and visit with our wonderful charge nurse. She sat down with me to help find closure with regard to what took place the night of October 2, 2013. She said by the time my wife had lost consciousness, the nurse on duty was in the room. Karen's heart had stopped and they began to administer medication to get her heart going again. At this point the nurse frantically informed the charge nurse that she was going to CODE!! Meaning she was going to "Announce CODE BLUE!" As the charge nurse made it to the room, the sight she describes to me is frightening. My dear wife of 25 years was non-responsive, and in the midst of a seizure. In her words, in all her years of nursing, she had never seen this on a regular floor. Medical records show that my wife had coded for four minutes. After hearing the charge nurse's story, I wonder if it could have been longer than four minutes. By the time I entered the room I was there to hear them count four minutes. So to this day, *I still really wonder*. That night I was not leaving my wife's side!

Chapter 17
The Raspberry Shirt

On the morning of October 2nd, I had gone home to freshen up and change clothes. As I searched for something to wear, the raspberry shirt called out to me. Earlier this year I purchased this bright colored shirt for the church picnic. A little out of the box for me because this shirt was bold and stood out. It was a no brainer. So, off I went back to the hospital sporting my raspberry shirt. A few nurses commented, "You really look good in that raspberry shirt". They said, "Not everyone can get away with wearing a raspberry shirt!" I kindly thanked them and my wife and I laughed. It was not until that night that the raspberry shirt took center stage.

Here is a portion of what Karen recalls: "As I was coming out of the first Code Blue I remember being fearful of my surroundings. I felt as though I was being attacked by people I'd never seen before. This is exactly how I felt... people literally attacking me in my sleep. But as I looked up I saw the raspberry shirt and knew it was my husband." It was then that I noticed my wife becoming more settled. As you recall, this is when the doctor took me by the hand and said, "Talk to her!" The raspberry shirt that I picked to wear that day was a God-send to me. Job said, **"The Lord knows the way I take."** I truly believe that it was the *Hand of God* that led me to choose the raspberry shirt. Not for the compliments but for what He foreknew was going to take place in our lives on that day. The raspberry shirt made it easy for my wife to locate me during a time that she desperately needed to find me. That is now my favorite shirt of all time. How fitting it is for this shirt to be the same color worn that represents National Breast Cancer Awareness Month, which is the month of October.

Chapter 18
Angel?

I must confess that I am not one to go off the beaten path in my Christian walk. I believe the *Phenomenon of God* and believe He can do what He wants, when He wants. *He is Sovereign, He is Creator.* But something unusual took place the first night my wife coded. As we were being ushered into room 12 of the Trauma ICU, there stood right in the middle of the floor a gentleman that never said one word during all of the commotion.

This well trained team of doctors and nurses are what I call, "Poetry in Motion". I will share this in the next segment of the book. The staff in this unit moved and operated with the utmost precision. But I could not help but notice, (by now you should know that I was well aware of my surroundings), a gentleman standing in the middle of the room. With what seemed liked ten to fifteen people moving about, no one disrupted him nor was his presence a disruption. He just stood there observing what was going on.

He never said one word; no one approached him or even asked anything of this gentleman. He silently observed everything that was going on. In my own thoughts, I wondered privately if this man was an Angel. Everyone else wore hospital staff attire. Not this gentleman, he was dressed in a green, black, and white striped shirt with a pair of khaki pants.

I recall as things began to calm down, someone asked if I needed anything. At first I said no and then I asked, "Yes, may I have some water?" I remember vividly looking right at this gentleman and sensed, as our eyes met… this man's purpose was far more than serving water. I seriously took it as though this individual was on *Divine Assignment* from God. I had a spiritual sense of security from this individual. I literally sensed that he was there to make sure we both were comfortable and that God would protect us. I had planned to keep this to myself because as I said, I'm not one to go off into visions and sightings. I am not saying that God can't do these things, I just try to stay balanced with scripture.

After a few days had passed and while Karen and I were talking, she asked me, "Who was that man standing in the room with the green striped shirt?" My mouth dropped. I knew all that had happened to her the night of October 2, 2013. For her to have flat-lined for some four minutes and experience being terrified by the entire trauma she went through, how in the world did she have the wherewithal to see the very same man that *I* had witnessed? Karen had the same testimony I had concerning this man's functions and actions that night, when she asked, "Honey, who was that man that stood right in the middle of the floor that did nothing but watch?" *Was this a manifestation of Isaiah 43:5a?* After my wife brought it up, we had to ask the staff about this gentleman. I must admit, we never saw that man again and the staff was not really sure who it was. They mentioned, "From time to time we have interns come in to observe."

Personally, Karen and I believe that the Lord not only sent her back that night, He provided an escort for her.

Chapter 19
"Poetry in Motion"

The Olympics have a water event called synchronized swimming. I confess that I'm not one to watch this event but have witnessed it in my lifetime. The choreography during this event is breathtaking. The practices for these events must be grueling and the hours spent, countless. Also, you can tell that the athletes participating are serious. Well, the hospital team that responds to a Code Blue is much the same, nothing short of "Poetry in Motion."

Not only is this team well synchronized, but they are also focused and mission minded. No disrespect to our men and women that serve this country but I liken this medical team's efforts to that of Army Rangers, Special Ops or SWAT Team members. These professionally trained individuals are a sight to behold.

When a code is sounded, these individuals are trained to go into action. They swiftly spring into action with one thing in mind… to save someone's life! In what seems like one seamless choreographed motion, as they arrive each one accesses the given situation with a trained professional approach. While they are accessing, they are also keenly aware that they are operating with minutes, and sometimes just seconds.

I have witnessed this team in action… twice, and both times I was impressed with their precision and cohesion. Each individual knew their role as well as their place. I noticed that each individual came from different locations throughout the hospital. They ascend upon their subject with the precision of heat seeking missiles that never miss their target. As they enter the given location, they each take their place or position to do what they do best. In this *all hands on deck operation*, someone is stationed at the top of the bed, the foot, and some on each side. In the background there are others observing, listening, and recording what is going on. One individual performs CPR, one waits with a defibrillator (which has to be set-up), and someone monitors the time when there is no heart rate or pulse.

While all this is taking place, the Trauma ICU Team (that may be located on a different floor) is preparing for the patient. When we arrived at the Trauma ICU, they were already in place (synchronized) to concur and hopefully reverse the CODE BLUE.

I want to personally thank the whole team for what they did (*twice*) for my wife. I'm not sure how many times these teams are called on but I do know now that when they are called, they come knowing what they are doing. I'm reminded of a scripture in the Bible that says, **"God will not forget your labor of love" Hebrew 6:10**. These teams of people may never be honored publically or on television, so I want to take a moment to honor each CODE BLUE Team Member that are camouflaged throughout our hospitals for the sole purpose of eliminating distractions of an otherwise *Quiet Place* (hospitals), and providing families with "MOMENTS" of joy. May God bless your Labor of Life (Love).

Thank You!

Chapter 20
I didn't get to say Good Bye

I want to share how quickly life can change for us. My hope is after you finish reading our story, you will find yourself re-evaluating the relationships you have in your life. When I hear someone say, *"life is short"* or *"here today, gone tomorrow"*, it now resonates as a true revelation in my heart. Before I go into the details of this defined revelation, I would like to share hind sight on my experience.

As I pen this Chapter, I am only two weeks removed from the most challenging two days of my life. When I walked into the room during Karen's first time coding, so many thoughts flooded my head. As I wrote earlier in our story, I seemed to be able to identify with everything that was taking place in room 662.

What I did not share in detail were my thoughts. After telling the nurse that attempted to deny me access, "THAT'S MY WIFE!" My mind was screaming, "This cannot be real!" How can one leave their loved one for a short moment and walk back in to this? I will never forget when I heard the doctor say, "We have no heart beat or pulse." I remember thinking, "Karen is DEAD! I DIDN'T GET TO SAY GOOD-BYE!" I didn't know how I was going to live without her. I heard myself saying the longest "Nooooooooooooooooo!" While at the same time covered in PEACE! Isaiah 43:5a. I was living in what the Bible describes as the Peace that passeth "All" understanding.

But even being in the Peace of God does not silence the human thought process. The thought process is subject to the Power of God's Peace that is present but God allows one to witness and experience His might in crisis. I can only equate the last statement through a Biblical passage in II Corinthians 12. The Apostle Paul had a thorn in his flesh. During his ordeal, his human side (like all of ours) begins appealing to God to get him out of the situation, in other words, SEND RELIEF!

Eventually, God answers Paul, resulting in one of the most powerful God/man moments recorded in scripture. God informs Paul that His grace was sufficient for Paul and that His strength was made perfect in weakness. Paul thought that removing the thorn would grant him relief, but Paul was granted relief by God telling him that His Grace was sufficient and that God's Power is made perfect when thorns are in our flesh. Notice that Paul begins to glory (rejoice) in his present state. Yes! Thorn still in, but understanding the purpose of the thorn and who was with him brought tremendous relief.

Paul discovered that as he gloried in his weakness, the power of God rested on him. So as Paul was experiencing his human crisis, he was living in the Power of God's peace that is manifested/revealed in crisis.

I would like to clear something up about when I asked God to send my wife back. It was not a demand. I remembered the broken man I was and would be if God decided to keep her. So out of a CRUSHED heart, I cried to the Lord. I did not tell God what to do, I simply asked, "SEND MY WIFE BACK, GOD." I will share more on this prayer later. Truth be told, my wife could easily be with God right now, and this resonates in my heart as I write. One thing she shared with me was that she was so weak, and all she wanted was her husband. In her words to the tech, "I NEED MY HUSBAND!"

I was not aware of her request when I entered room 662 that evening. But I can only imagine if the Lord decided to take her, and eventually discovered that she wanted me in her last moments… Whew! I would have to live with the pain that she wanted me but I wasn't there for her. *Let's not even go there!* I am so glad that the Lord has given me a chance to be there. I don't know what the future holds but one thing I am determined to do is be there for Karen. Not just in moments of crisis, but every chance I have. My niece, Lashawn, said to me while my wife was in the hospital, "People thought you all were close before, what will they think now?"

My hope is that I will not have to live with the thought that I was not there when she needed me the most. The next segment sealed it for me; I hope it does for you.

Chapter 21
NOT ONCE, BUT TWICE!

This moment will forever be etched in my mind. I have been through many things in my life. Never knowing my mother because I was 5 years old when she passed away, and as Pastor seeing many painful events in the lives of the many members of my Church. But sitting only two feet away from my wife and seeing her flat-line went deep.

The night after Karen coded the first time, I was determined to be by her side until we left that hospital together. On the night of October 2, 2013 (First Code Blue), we spent that night in the Trauma ICU. My wife's heart and other vitals were monitored 24/7. During the night, we spent much of the time in conversation because she was afraid to close her eyes. Our conversation mostly centered on the importance of life and how we would spend it together.

Karen was not comfortable closing her eyes and I understood why… so I sang, read and prayed until morning. I would not take my eyes off the monitor that displayed her vitals. Each heartbeat being my main focus, I did not sleep a wink that night, sleeping just didn't matter. *I was just so glad that she was alive!*

I remember Karen with three IV's in her arm, a precautionary measure just in case they had to give fluids in an emergency (part of the synchronization). I remember the pain I felt seeing her with needles in her arms, pain from her abdomen that also ran through her body as a result of the CPR, electrical shock from the defibrillator and, again, the level of fear she had that prevented her from closing her eyes. Every now and then her body would uncontrollably twitch. Sometimes there was a blank stare and I could tell her mind was trying to process all that she had been through.

As she fought to keep her eyes open, she would call out to me to make sure I was still there. "I'm here baby, I'm right here! I'm not going anywhere! Ok?" With that assurance she would nod for a few moments and repeat the experience again.

As I heard her unconscious groans and her irregular breathing, I found myself with tears under my chin throughout that night. My heart ached for my wife! It is so painful when you are helpless for your loved one. Not being able to run interference for Karen ate at me. I could not believe this had happened to Karen, and what we thought was just a routine visit to the hospital turned out to be the most challenging days of our lives.

Early in the morning Karen and I were talking, while from time to time my eyes would glance at the monitor. I was sitting right beside her bed, only 2 feet away from her. At 8:00AM she told me that she was dizzy. Not even a second after that statement, I saw my wife's eyes roll back in her head and she started to seize. My eyes went to the monitor right away and what I witnessed on that monitor still leaves me speechless. The top line that monitors the patient's heart went from 88 to 134 to 194 in less than a second. I cried out, "MY WIFE IS CODING! MY WIFE IS CODING! MY WIFE IS CODING!"

I could hear in the background the synchronized team fast approaching with precision. As they took their positions, I heard one of the nurses say, "Sir, you are going to have to move." I kindly responded, "I will so you all can do what you do best." As I moved towards the corner of the room I noticed a nurse pulling out a chair and asked me if I would like to sit down. She then hesitantly asked, "Do you want to see this?"

Based on how she asked her question, I wondered if I was supposed to say no. Instead, as I opened my mouth, I whispered to her, "I want to see my wife!" As the team did their job, I did mine. I called my Father in heaven. I simply said, "Lord, don't take her, Lord, don't take her." As I was observing the Code team for the second time, I noticed each team member was in place to do what they were trained to do. When I say awesome... It was truly awesome to witness how this team worked in sync with each other. Every member was in accord with the others and striving for the same purpose… and that was to save Karen's life.

I noticed after they performed CPR, they immediately applied the defibrillator. As my wife's body jarred from the shock, she began to breathe and I could see her stomach rise.

I heard a nurse say, "She's breathing," so as to prevent the individual from shocking her again. When I heard her say, "She's breathing," I called out to my wife and said, "Honey, I'm here! Baby, I'm here!" When this happened, it seemed like the staff opened up a pathway for me to get to Karen. As long as I live, I will never forget what happened when our eyes made contact. My wife, in the midst of her fearful state had the most trusting, calm, relaxed look on her face. I could tell she wanted to know what had happened, she did ask, but she just trusted me and she nodded her head as if to say, "OK," after I told her that they were helping her.

I believe Isaiah 43:5a covered us throughout this whole ordeal. It is still with us as we continue down our road to complete recovery. There is no doubt that my wife and I will forever be changed by these events. Only God knows the plans and purpose for why He has allowed Karen to die twice and lived to tell about it. Wherever He leads us, it will be for His Glory and His Glory alone.

Chapter 22
The Facts!

There is so much more that I can share about these miraculous events that took place in our lives. Like, the night of her second time coding, Karen could not get comfortable. We had at least a dozen pillows on her bed to try and relieve her of her misery. This is one of the nights that the small of her back was in excruciating pain, with tears flowing from her eyes she said, "I can't get comfortable, if I can just get some relief in the small of my back." I went to the opposite side of her bed and I put my fists together and gently maneuvered them into the small of her back. I asked her if this helped and she responded by nodding yes, "That feels perfect." I don't know how long I stood there but I do know that she was able to finally drift off to sleep as I sang song after song with my hands supporting her back.

A few days after my wife was stable, I took a moment to speak with the chief physician as well as one of the nurses that had been on duty the night we came into the Trauma ICU. <u>First</u>, I will start with my conversation with the nurse. She informed me that the day my wife coded the second time (the time I called out, "MY WIFE IS CODING!") it was twenty seconds after I called out that it registered on their monitors outside of Karen's room. *TWENTY SECONDS!* <u>Second</u>, the same nurse said that in all her years of nursing, she had never seen anyone come out of *V-Fib* not having any broken bones, not on a ventilator for two or three days, and being able to speak like nothing ever happened. Karen came back talking like nothing ever happened.

Let me explain *V-Fib*. This is short for *Ventricular Fibrillation*. Brace yourself! This is when the bottom of the heart just stops and shakes, no blood is being pumped out of the arteries. As a matter of fact, no blood is being pumped at all. This is what happened to my wife during the second time she coded. The first time her blood sugar bottomed out which also lead to Cardiac Arrest.

<u>Third</u>, the nurse declared that Karen is a Miracle.

I spoke to the charge nurse on duty when she flat-lined on the sixth floor, room 662. She shared with me that, "In all my years of nursing, I have never seen what took place with your wife on a regular hospital floor." I quote, "Pastor, I was scared to death for your wife. When I came into the room, she was already having a seizure. We did what we could to start getting a regular heartbeat. She is a Miracle!" As I continued to get closure on what happened, I then asked her a question that I knew the answer to but wanted to make sure that I was sharing accurate information. The question I asked her was when someone codes, are they considered to have died. She answered, "YES, YOUR WIFE WAS DEAD!" She then said, "I will forever be connected with you and your wife."

And, finally, the chief physician. I sat down and asked him, **"What really happened to my wife?"** His response to me was, "Let me give you the *medical* terms first, then the *Spiritual* second. The first time your wife coded, it was for FOUR MINUTES, and the second time your wife coded was for SIX MINUTES!" He broke down how the electrolytes in the body function and how if they are off it causes the heart to become angry. He shared with me that my wife's body was completely depleted of all its electrolytes. He shared that her potassium levels were extremely low and after he shared some other details, he then turned to the Spiritual and these are his words to me, "Pastor, your **PRAYERS BROUGHT HER BACK!!!"**

Knowing what I know now, I am truly in AWE of how God can take an individual and allow them to die for four minutes and then six minutes. No oxygen, no blood or breath, then bring them back to life and they are the same person! *ONLY GOD* can do something like that! You see, we have heard it said from medical professionals that three minutes of no oxygen to the brain can leave an individual with a degree of brain damage.

Karen did not suffer any brain damage, her motor skills are intact, her language skills are the same, and she has total recall of recent as well as all past events in her life!

In addition to our miracle(s), Karen now has this wonderful *glow* on her countenance. (Like Moses face shined as he traveled down from Mt. Sinai, See Exodus 34:29) Most of all, SHE IS STILL PRAISING THE LORD JESUS CHRIST! For this I am ever so grateful!

Chapter 23
Never the same

Finally, as my wife lay recovering in the hospital, there were three or four occasions in which a Code Blue was sounded over the intercom. No longer silent in our world, we immediately began to pray in sync with the Code Blue team that we knew was on a mission to save a life, and that their mission would be accomplished.

I hope in some way, our story has helped you to know that there is a GOD that answers prayers and gives second and third chances; even if it means bringing one back to life. I am convinced that no matter how bad circumstances look, ***it's never too late for God.***

One last thing... as I was sitting at Karen's bed side two nights before her release, a Code Blue sounded over the intercom; I immediately began to pray. My wife was startled because she thought they were calling out her room number. She was actually wondering if she was coding and just didn't know it yet. After praying, I looked up at the nurse's message board and my eyes landed on my wife's room number (at this time she was in the heart hospital room #5086). The Code Blue called on this night was for the fourth floor, room #4086. I was stunned for a moment when it finally sunk in; I realized that someone needed resuscitation directly under our room. I could not believe that a Code Blue was lurking so close. Today I still wonder the outcome of the Code Blue that hovered so close to *my wife's life* that night... or even *my life*.

Pastor Gary L. Pleasant
1st Lady Karen J. Pleasant (My Triple Miracle from God)

1) May 28, 1988 @ 4:00PM
2) October 2, 2013 @ 9:15PM
3) October 3, 2013 @ 8:15AM

Prayer: Lord Jesus, we thank You for defeating death over 2000 years ago. We also take this time to thank you for defeating death twice in my wife's life. We are forever grateful to You for your wondrous ways. Allow the lives we now live to bring glory to your Name forever. Praise your Holy Name!!! Amen

We Love You
Be Blessed

The following Poem was given to Mrs Baich after reading our story....

Code Blue

What does Code Blue really mean to you?
Is this truly the time to consider living your life anew?
Should this be the moment you first hit your knees in prayer?
And is this the time you'll wait until to discover God is *ALWAYS* there?

Does a Code Blue only occur on distant hospital floors?
Or could it also happen during trials behind a questioning heart's closed doors?
In the moments of distress, hurt, and profound pain...
Maybe it takes a "Code Blue" to turn a life to God again?

And for those that have faith and know there is more,
They are ready and able when a "Code Blue" knocks on their door!
To have a loving conversation with God about their needs,
Then rest in their faith to see where Our Savior then leads.

As these moments rest on my heart I look into His sky,
To ponder these moments of life and death and *know* He wants us to try.
I see gentle clouds of white and crystal clearness through and through...
I breathe His sweet air and feel wind sung by the angels... all mixed in His color of blue.

Dear God please be with us during our good times and stress.
Please keep us calm and in your care to help us do our best.
Please show us how to be strong for others and keep our focus clearly on you...
Please prepare us for those times in life when we lovingly cry out, "CODE BLUE!"

Denise McCormick Baich

Story through Pictures

My Big Sister

My Big Brother

Together

Just Us!

Still Us!

Always Us!

Story through Pictures

Place I sat in the Lobby

Another view of Lobby

Comfort Scriptures Lobby Wall

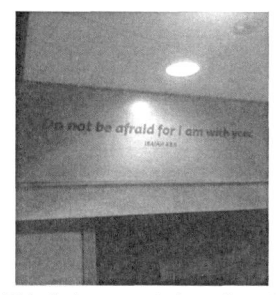

This Scripture carried me through
The darkest two days of my life…

Corner I rounded to Room 662

Corridor to Room 662. Right past
3rd ceiling light

Story through Pictures

First Code Blue Room 662

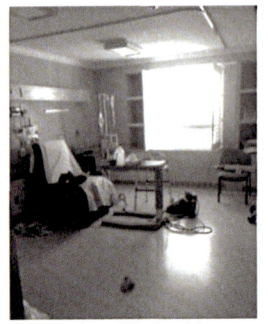

Empty, but filled with memories

Written in 662 before ever coding

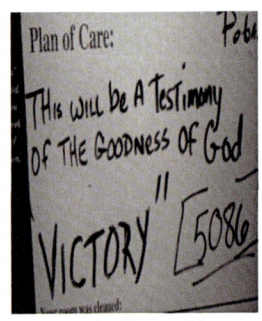

Written by Pastor Pleasant in Trauma `Unit

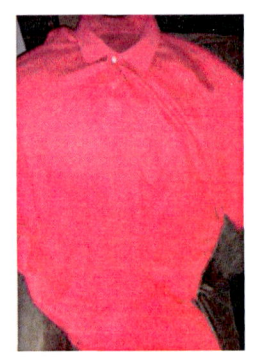

The Raspberry Shirt

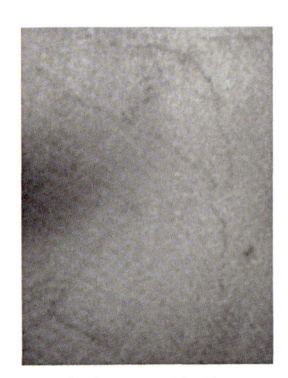

Marks from Defibrillator

First Sunday Returning to Church Thank You Jesus!

Mom, you have always been there for me. Thank you for calling & praying with me moments before I coded on Oct 2, 2013. Love you, Mom.

Special Thanks!

Our Families
Pastor and 1st Lady David Baker
New Direction Christian Church
Bishop and 1st Lady James Holloway
Solomons Temple Church
Pastor and 1st Lady Roderrick Walker
Grace Bible Church
Pastor and 1st Lady John Sykes
Grace Community Church
Bishop and 1st Lady Lawrence Wooten
Williams Temple Church of God in Christ
Pastor and 1st Lady (Dr)Julius Sims
Word of Life Fellowship
Pastor and 1st Lady TD Stubblefield
First Baptist Church of Chesterfield
Pastor and 1st Lady James Smith
Corinthian Baptist Church
Bishop and 1st Lady Calvin Scott
Beleivers Temple

Stephanie Chatman Adkins (our sister) for having Church with LadyP; Streaming live services, And your creative gift baskets from **Gift Baskets Etc.. 314 313 3742** Thanks Al Adkins & Mom Chatman for sharing her.

Denise McCormick Baich (Sister D) Thank you for helping edit this book. Thank you for your poem (Code Blue).For making our appointments at "CleanSpa". We pray that you continue expressing God's goodness through Poetry/ Your best days are coming. Author Holy Hiccups, book of Poetry

Mr Kevin Baich You are a Great Man! Thanks for allowing your wife to share her gift that enabled us to finish this project

Dr Andrea Hill (Lady P's Best Friend) You were THERE!
Lillie Dumas Branch Mgr Commerce Bank
Nurse A.Jackson, Her private duty nurse. Thanks

To ALL that shopped, sat, cooked (especially our Sunday dinner specialist), preached, taught, traveled and prayed…**THANK YOU! THANK YOU! THANK YOU!**

Other Books & Poems
by
Pastor Gary Pleasant

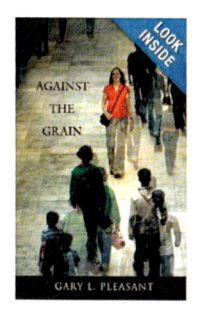

Against the Grain: a call to live life against popular culture thinking.

The bible is clear that the days of Noah will be repeated. Are we seeing the last days?

Series of self-examining, challenging writings; if you want to be real with yourself, Take a Snapshot COMING SOON Snapshot 3

Coming Soon!

Unforgiveness, Let it Go! "It's like you taking poison and hoping someone else dies"

They Did What was Right in Their own Eyes "When the boss is away, the mice will play" The dangers of being left to ourselves!

Comfort: The Father is Watching Written to comfort every parent that has lost a child.

Poems by Pastor Pleasant

"From Sore to Soar"
"My Place of Prayer"
"I Want Out!"

Contact Information:pastorpnlcc@gmail.com